J. J Lansdell

The Biblical Catechism

Designed for Sabbath Schools

J. J Lansdell

The Biblical Catechism
Designed for Sabbath Schools

ISBN/EAN: 9783743325067

Manufactured in Europe, USA, Canada, Australia, Japa

Cover: Foto ©ninafisch / pixelio.de

Manufactured and distributed by brebook publishing software (www.brebook.com)

J. J Lansdell

The Biblical Catechism

BIBLICAL CATECHISM,

DESIGNED FOR

SABBATH SCHOOLS.

BY

REV. J. J. LANSDELL.

NO. 1.

RALEIGH:
BIBLICAL RECORDER PRINT.
1863.

Entered according to Act of Congress, in the year 1863,
By J. J. LANSDELL,
In the Clerk's Office of the District Court of the Confederate States, for the District of Pamlico,
North Carolina.

TO THE
SABBATH SCHOOLS
CONNECTED WITH THE
CHURCHES OF CHRIST IN THE
CONFEDERATE STATES.
THIS VOLUME IS
RESPECTFULLY DEDICATED
WITH THE HUMBLE HOPE THAT IT MAY BE
OF SOME SERVICE TO THOSE WHO ARE
ENGAGED IN TEACHING
RELIGIOUS TRUTH TO THE
RISING GENERATION.

PREFACE.

This work, which is now offered to the public, has been called forth by the exigencies of the times. The scarcity of Sabbath School text books since the beginning of the present war has been a serious drawback in the efficiency of Sabbath School instruction, and the scarcity of Scripture question books has been especially felt. It is hoped that this volume will supply, in part, the present demand. In its preparation, my object has been to present plain truths in a plain manner, so that the young student may be instructed instead of puzzled.

In teaching, the student should be required to commit to memory such passages of Scripture as are referred to, as well as those copied in the lesson, so as to impress on the youthful memory such Scripture truth as will be the foundation of a sound theology in time to come.

That this work may be of service to those who are engaged in the great work of Sabbath School instruction, is the sincere desire and humble prayer of

THE AUTHOR.

RALEIGH, N. C., May, 1863.

LESSON I

Creation of Man.

Ques. Who made you?

Ans. God.

In what image was man created?

In the image of God.

Genesis 1 : 27. "God created man in his own image, in the image of God created he him."

Out of what was man formed?

Out of the dust of the earth.

Did his soul come from the dust of the earth?

No; his soul came more directly from God.

Genesis 2 : 7. "And the Lord God formed man of the dust of the ground, and breathed into his nostrils the breath of life; and man became a living soul."

In what natural condition was man created?

"Male and female created he them," Gen. 1 : 27.

What was man's relative position to other portions of God's creation?

He was superior to all other.

Gen. 1 : 28. "And God blessed them, and God said unto them, Be fruitful and multiply, and replenish the earth, and subdue it and have dominion over the fish of the sea, and over the foul of the air, and over every living thing that moveth upon the earth."

What was man's moral condition?

It was good.

Gen. 1: 31. "And God saw every thing that he had made and behold it was very good."

'Tis by thy power, Almighty God,
 The heavens and earth were made;
Thy hand the starry heavens spread,
 And earth's foundations laid.

The teeming millions of the sea,
 And creeping things of earth,
At thy command, Eternal God,
 Were ushered into birth.

Then chief o'er all thy works below,
 Man, honored man was made;
His soul with God's pure image stamped,
 With innocence arrayed.

Completed now the mighty work,
 God, his creation viewed;
And, pleased with all that he had made,
 Pronounced it very good.

LESSON II.

Fall and Depravity of Man.

Ques. What is the chief purpose for which man was created?

Ans. To love and to serve God.

Deut. 6: 5. "Thou shalt love the Lord thy God with all thy heart, and with all thy soul, and with all thy might,".... "and him only shalt thou serve." Mat. 4: 10.

Does man answer this great end of his creation?

He does not; he hates God, and refuses to serve him.

Romans 8: 7. "The carnal mind is enmity against God." Ps. 53: 2, 3. "God looked down from heaven upon the children of men, to see if there were any that did understand, that did seek God. Every one of them is gone back; .... there is none that doeth good, no, not one."

What would you say of man, seeing that this is his condition?

I would say that he is a sinner.

Are all men sinners?

They are; "for all have sinned, and come short of the glory of God." Rom. 3: 23.

What constitutes man a sinner?

The transgression of the law.

"Whosoever committeth sin transgresseth also the law; for sin is the transgression of the law." 1 John 3: 4.

What is meant by transgressing the law?

It means a refusing to do those things required by the law.

Whose law has man refused to obey?
The law of God, and has thereby become a sinner against God.

Does God hold man accountable for his sins?
He does; and unless he repent he must perish, and be punished forever. Luke 13 : 3. "Except ye repent, ye shall all likewise perish." Matt. 25 : 46. "These shall go away into everlasting punishment."

How sad our state by nature is!
  Our sin, how deep it stains!
And Satan binds our captive minds
  Fast in his slavish chains.

But, hark! a voice of sovereign love!
  'Tis Christ's inviting word—
" Ho! ye despairing sinners, come,
  And trust upon the Lord."

My soul obeys th' almighty call,
  And runs to this relief;
I would believe thy promise, Lord;
  O, help my unbelief.

To the dear fountain of thy blood,
  Incarnate God, I fly;
Here let me wash my spotted soul.
  From stains of deepest dye.

A guilty, weak, and helpless worm,
  On thy kind arms I fall;
Be thou my strength and righteousness,
  My Saviour and my all.

LESSON III

Fall and Depravity

Ques. Are little children sinners?

Ans. They are.

What makes them sinners?

They are sinners because they are of a sinful race.

What are some of the first developments of the sinful disposition of children?

Disobedience to parents.

Is it wrong for children to disobey their parents?

It is; because parents are more likely to know what is good for their children than children are themselves.

Can you give any farther evidence that it is wrong and sinful for children to disobey their parents?

I can. Exodus 20: 12. "Honor thy father and thy mother, that thy days may be long upon the land which the Lord thy God giveth thee."

Can you give any farther evidence of the sinful disposition of children?

I can. Ps. 51: 5. "Behold, I was shapen in iniquity; and in sin did my mother conceive me." Job. 14: 4. "Who can bring a clean thing out of an unclean? Not one."

What do these passages seem to teach?

They teach that the children of sinners are likewise sinners.

Who were the first sinners?

Adam and Eve, who were the first man and woman, and from whom all other men have sprung.

How did Adam and Eve become sinners?

By disobeying God.

What command did they disobey?

"The Lord God commanded man, saying of every tree of the garden thou mayest freely eat; but of the tree of knowledge of good and evil thou shalt not eat." Gen. 2: 16, 17.

Was God displeased with Adam because of his disobedience.

He was; so much so that he drove him out of the garden of Eden, and placed obstructions to his entering it again. See Gen. 3: 23, 24.

Is God displeased with all wicked persons?

He is. "God is angry with the wicked every day." Ps. 7: 11.

Did the whole race of man become sinners by reason of Adam's transgression?

They did. "Wherefore as by one man sin entered into the world, and death by sin; and so death passed upon all men, for that all have sinned." Rom. 5: 12.

Since death is the consequence of sin, is it not a dreadful thing to sin against God?

Lord we are vile conceived in sin,
And born unholy and unclean;

Sprung from the man whose guilty fall
Corrupts the race, and taints us all.

Soon as we draw our infant breath,
The seeds of sin grow up for death;
Thy law demands a perfect heart,
But we 're defiled in every part.

Great God, create our hearts anew,
And form our spirits pure and true:
O, make us wise betimes, to see
Our danger and our remedy.

LESSON IV.

Guilt and Depravity.

Ques. From what we have seen of the teachings of the Scriptures, what would you say of the condition of man?

Ans. I would say that his condition is most wretched and helpless.

Why is his condition wretched?

Because he is under the curse of God.

What is that curse?

"The soul that sinneth it shall die," Ezekiel 18 : 4, and since all men are sinners, all rest under this curse.

Why is man's condition helpless?

Because he is in a condition from which it is impossible for him to relieve himself.

Can you explain this?

I think I can. We can get into difficulties much easier than we can get out of them; I could fall down a precipice that I could not climb up again.

Do we experience any of the evil consequences of sin in this world?

We do; all our sorrows, afflictions and toils; all pestilences, famines and wars, are the results of sin.

What were the temporal curses which God pronounced against Adam when he sinned?

"Cursed is the ground for thy sake; in sorrow shalt thou eat of it all the days of thy life; thorns also and thistles shall it bring forth to thee; and thou shalt eat of the herb of the field: in the sweat of thy face shalt thou eat bread, till thou return to the ground; for out of it wast thou taken; for dust thou art, and unto dust shalt thou return." Gen. 3: 17, 18, 19.

Have mankind universally experienced these calamities?

They have in every particular.

Are temporal calamities the only evil effects of sin which men experience?

No, by no means. They are but the beginning, and admonish us of an eternity of misery after death.

Can you give any Scripture proof of a future state of misery and torment?

"The wicked shall be turned into hell, and all the nations that forget God. Ps. 9: 17. "The rich man died also, and was buried; and in hell he lifted up his eyes, being in torment." Luke 16 : 22, 23.

What do these terrible consequences of sin teach us?

They teach us God's great abhorrence of sin, and admonish us to seek a remedy for sin.

What does Paul say of the natural condition of man as a sinner?

That he is "dead in trespasses and sins" Eph. 2 : 1.

Can a dead thing bring itself to life?

It can not.

Can sinners, therefore, who are spiritually dead, restore themselves to spiritual life?

They can not; this must be done by the power of God. Eph. 2 : 4, 5.

If we are not restored to spiritual life while in this world, what must our condition be in the world to come?

We must experience forever all the terrible consequences of that spiritual death in which we are now involved by reason of our sins.

Have you any evidence that you have been restored to spiritual life?

How is our nature spoiled by sin!
Yet nature ne'er hath found
The way to make the conscience clean,
Or heal the painful wound.

In vain we seek for peace with God
By methods of our own;

Jesus, there's nothing but thy blood
  Can bring us near thy throne.

The threatenings of thy broken law.
  Impress our souls with dread;
If God his sword of vengeance draw,
  It strikes our spirits dead.

But thine illustrious sacrifice
  Hath answered these demands,
And peace and pardon from the skies
  Come down by Jesus' hands.

'Tis by thy death we live, O Lord;
  'Tis on thy cross we rest:
Forever be thy love adored,
  Thy name forever blest.

LESSON V.

Christ, our Saviour.

Ques. We have seen the wretched condition of man as a sinner; is there any way by which he can be saved from his sins and restored to the favor of God?

Ans. There is; "God so loved the world that he gave his only begotten Son, that whosoever believeth on him should not perish, but have everlasting life." John 3: 16.

What would you call this announcement?

I would call it the *gospel*.

What does the word *gospel* mean?

It means *good news*.

Can you explain how this announcement is good news to the sinner?

I think I can. If a man were perishing with hunger, and it should be announced to him that some kind friend had offered to feed him, and thus to save him from death, I would consider it good news to the perishing man; and so the announcement of salvation to guilty sinners is good news to them.

What caused God to provide salvation for sinners?

His love for them—"God *so loved* the world."

What is meant by the expression "the world"?

The men in the world, who are sinners.

What did God do to provide salvation for sinners?

He gave his only begotten Son.

Was not this a great gift?

It was. I do not see how a greater gift could have been made.

What would you say, then, of the love which moved the Almighty in bestowing so great a gift?

I would say that the love was equal to the gift.

Did God love us because we were lovely?

No; he did not, but because we were helpless, and he pitied us.

Do you suppose that any thing less than the gift of God's Son would have effected our salvation?

I suppose it would not, or God, in his wisdom, would have provided it.

Do you suppose that any thing less than the gift of God's Son would have been a full expression of God's love to us?

I suppose it would not, or he would have given expressions of his love only through other means.

What would you say, then, of the gift of God's son for our redemption?

I would say that it is the highest expression of God's love.

Ought we not to love God, in return for the great love wherewith he loves us?

Do mankind generally love God?

They do not; but on the contrary, they hate him, and despise his laws.

Do you love God?

Plunged in a gulf of dark despair,
 We wretched sinners lay,
Without one cheerful beam of hope,
 Or spark of glimmering day.

With pitying eyes the Prince of grace
 Beheld our helpless grief;
He saw, and—O, amazing love:—
 He flew to our relief.

Down from the shining seats above,
 With joyful haste he fled,
Entered the grave in mortal flesh,
 And dwelt among the dead.

O, for this love, let rocks and hills
 Their lasting silence break,
And all harmonious human tongues
 The Saviour's praises speak.

Angels assist our mighty joys;
Strike all your harps of gold,
But when you raise your highest notes,
His love can ne'er be told.

LESSON VI.

Advent of Christ.

How did the Son of God make his advent into the world?

He was born of the virgin Mary, Mat. 1: 23.

Where was he born?

In Bethlehem, in the country of Judea. Mat. 2: 1.

By what names is he usually called?

Jesus, Christ, and Emmanuel.

What does the name Jesus mean?

It means *Saviour.* "And thou shalt call his name Jesus; for he shall save his people from their sins." Mat. 1: 21.

What does the name Christ mean?

It means the anointed.

What does the name Emmanuel mean?

It means, "God with us." Mat. 1: 23.

Under what circumstances was Christ born?

Under those of the deepest poverty. He was wrapped in swaddling clothes, and laid in a manger, Luke 2: 7.

What kind of clothes are "swaddling clothes," and what is a manger?

"Swaddling clothes" are very mean garments—perhaps they were used to rub down the beasts of the stable with; and a manger is a trough or box in which beasts are fed.

What great moral lesson do we learn from these humble circumstances connected with the birth of Christ?

We learn that God's richest jewels on earth are sometimes concealed from public gaze by the deepest poverty, and that we should not be led away by a fair outward show in religion.

Who announced the birth of Christ?

The angel of God. Luke 2: 9.

To whom was the announcement made?

To the shepherds, who were watching their flock by night. Luke 2: 8.

What was the announcement which the angel made?

"Behold I bring you good tidings of great joy, which shall be to all people.—For unto you is born this day in the city of David a Saviour, which is Christ the Lord." Luke 2: 10, 11.

What else appeared to the shepherds?

"And suddenly there was with the angel a multitude of the heavenly hosts praising God, and saying, Glory to God in the highest, on earth peace, good will toward men." Luke 2: 13, 14.

What other remarkable occurrence took place at the birth of Christ?

A star was seen by certain wise men of the east, and it went before them, until it stood over the place where Jesus was.—Matt. 2: 9.

When these wise men came into the presence of the infant Jesus, what did they do?

They fell down and worshipped him, and opened their treasures, and presented unto him gifts of gold, frankincense, and myrrh.—Matt. 2: 11.

Ought we not also to worship Christ, and to make offerings unto him?

We certainly ought, and it is very sinful to refuse to do so.

But how can we now make offerings unto Christ?

By contributing of our money and other substance to support religion.

Do you worship Christ, and contribute to the cause of religion?

Hark! the herald angels sing,
"Glory to the new-born King;
Peace on earth, and mercy mild;
God and sinners reconciled."

Joyful, all ye nations, rise;
Join the triumph of the skies;
With th' angelic host proclaim,
"Christ is born in Bethlehem."

See, he lays his glory by,
Born, that man no more may die—
Born to raise the sons of earth—
Born to give them second birth.

Hail, the holy Prince of Peace!
Hail, the Sun of Righteousness!
Light and life to all he brings,
Risen with healing in his wings.

Let us, then, with angels sing,
"Glory to the new-born King;
Peace on earth, and mercy mild;
God and sinners reconciled."

LESSON VII.

Herod's Wickedness.

Ques. Who was King over Judea when Christ was born?

Ans. Herod. Matt. 2: 1.

What decree did Cæsar Augustus put forth " in those days"?

A decree "that all the world should be taxed." Luke 2: 1.

Who was this Cæsar Augustus?

He was the Roman king, and is usually called Augustus Cæsar.

What had he to do with Judea?

Judea was, at that time, a province under the Roman government, and enjoyed its protection, and therefore had to pay tax to Cæsar.

Was Herod a Roman?

No, he was a Jew, and was appointed by Cæsar as king over Judea.

By what title was Christ called by the wise men of the east?

He was called the "King of the Jews." Mat. 2 : 2.

How was Herod affected when he heard of the birth of Christ, and of the title which had been given him?

He was troubled. Mat. 2 : 3.

What do you suppose was the cause of Herod's trouble?

Perhaps he feared that the government of the Jews would be taken from him and given to Christ.

What secret request did Herod make of the wise men respecting Christ.

"He sent them to Bethlehem, and said, Go and search diligently for the young child; and when ye have found him, bring me word again, that I may come and worship him also." Mat 2 : 8

Did the wise men return to Herod?

They did not, but, "being warned of God in a dream that they should not return to Herod; they departed into their own country another way." Mat. 2 : 12.

Do you think that Herod desired to worship Christ as he said?

I do not, but he wished to see him, no doubt, that he might have an opportunity to kill him.

Was not this a very wicked thing in Herod?

It was, and he must have been a very wicked man.

Herod being disappointed in his wicked purpose, what did he next do?

"Then Herod, when he saw that he was mocked of the wise men, was exceeding wroth, and sent forth, and slew all the children that were in Bethlehem, and in the coasts thereof, from two years old and under, according to the time which he had diligently inquired of the wise men." Matt. 2 : 16.

Where was Christ when this wicked deed was done?

He was away down in Egypt.

How came he there?

"The angel of the Lord appeared to Joseph in a dream, saying, Arise, and take the young child and his mother, and flee into Egypt, and be thou there till I bring thee word." Matt. 2 : 13.

What great moral truth do we learn in the account here given of the remarkable preservation of the infant Jesus from the murderous designs of Herod?

We learn that he who strives against the Almighty shall not prosper in the end.

Are you striving against him?

> Joy to the world! the Lord is come
> Let earth receive her King;
> Let every heart prepare him room,
> And heaven and nature sing,

Joy to the earth! the Saviour reigns.
Let men their songs employ;
While fields, and floods, rocks, hills, and plains,
Repeat the sounding joy.

No more let sins and sorrows grow,
Nor thorns infest the ground;
He comes to make his blessings flow
Far as the curse is found.

He rules the world with truth and grace,
And makes the nations prove
The glories of his righteousness,
And wonders of his love.

LESSON VIII.

John the Baptist.

Ques. Who was the official forerunner of Christ?

Ans. John the Baptist.

What was his mission?

To prepare the way of the Lord, or " to make ready a people prepared for the Lord." Mark 1: 3.

How did John fulfill his mission?

By preaching the doctrine of repentance and baptizing those who believed his teachings. Matt. 3: 2, 5, 6.

What was John's great proclamation?

" Repent ye, for the kingdom of heaven is at hand." Matt. 3: 2.

What is meant here by " the kingdom of heaven"?

It means the reign of Christ in the great work of salvation.

What is said, Mark 1 : 1, of the mission of John?

That it is "the beginning of the gospel of the Son of God."

To whom did John direct the minds of the people?

To Christ, "saying, there cometh one mightier than I after me, the latchet of whose shoes I am not worthy to stoop down and unloose." Mark 1 : 7, Luke 3 : 16.

Should not all preachers of the gospel imitate the example of John in this respect?

They certainly ought. Christ should be the great theme of their preaching.

Did John baptize all the people in Judea, or all those who came to his baptism?

He did not; for he called the Pharisees and Sadducees, who came to his baptism, a "generation of vipers," Matt. 3 : 7, and Christ says "the Pharisees and lawyers rejected the counsel of God against themselves, being not baptized of him." Luke 7 : 30.

What, then, does Luke mean, chap. 3 : 21, when he says, "Now when all the people were baptized"?

He must mean this: when all the people who submitted to the ordinance of baptism, were baptized.

In what light did the people look upon John?

They regarded him as a prophet, and

some wondered if he were not the Christ. Matt. 13 : 5, Luke 3 : 15.

What was Christ's testimony in regard to John?

"Among those that are born of women, there is not a greater prophet than John the Baptist." Luke 7 : 28.

What did John say of himself?

"He said, I am the voice of one crying in the wilderness, make straight the way of the Lord." John 1 : 23.

Where did John baptize?

In the river of Jordan, Mark 1 : 5, and "in Enon near to Salim, because there was much water there." John 3 : 23.

Does it require much water for baptism?

It seems that it required "much water" when John baptized, and I would think that it requires the same now.

What did the people do whom John baptized?

They confessed their sins. Mark 1 : 5.

What is the confession of sins evidence of?

It is evidence of penitence.

What seems to be the character of those whom John baptized?

They seem to be penitent believers.

How was John clothed, and what was his diet?

"John was clothed with camel's hair, and with a girdle of skin about his loins; and he did eat locusts and wild honey." Mark 1: 6. His garments were, therefore, coarse and uncomely, and his diet such as the wilderness afforded.

What important lesson do we learn from these circumstances in his life?

We learn that ministers of the gospel whose circumstances in life are humble, should not be despised on that account.

" Repent !" the voice celestial cries ;
  No longer dare delay ;
The soul that scorns the mandate dies,
  And meets a fiery day.

No more the sovereign eye of God
  O'erlooks the crimes of men ;
His heralds now are sent abroad
  To warn the world of sin.

Bow ere the awful trumpet sound,
  And call you to his bar ;
His mercy knows th' appointed bound,
  And turns to vengeance there.

Amazing love, that yet will call,
  And yet prolong our days!
Our hearts subdued by goodness, fall,
  And weep, and love, and praise.

LESSON IX.

Baptism of Christ.

Ques. Was Christ baptized?
Ans. He was.

By whom was he baptized?
By John the Baptist.

Where was Christ baptized?
In the water of the river Jordan.

From whence did Christ come when he applied to John for baptism?

He came from Nazareth of Galilee, which is supposed to be a distance of about thirty three miles from Jordan. Mark 1: 9.

What was Chrsit's mode of traveling?
On foot, or walking.

Why was Christ baptized? had he any sins to confess or to repent of?

He had not; but he was baptized "to fulfill all righteousness." Mat. 3: 15.

What "righteousness" was fulfilled in the baptism of Christ?

The ordinance of baptism being observed by him, he acknowledged it to be of divine appointment, and thereby laid an example for his people in all coming time.

When Jesus was baptized, what remarkable occurrence took place as he went up out of the water?

"The heavens were opened unto him, and

he saw the Spirit of God descending like a dove, and lighting upon him; and lo, a voice from heaven, saying, this is my beloved Son, in whom I am well pleased." Mat 3 : 16, 17.

Did any besides Christ see the descent of the Spirit upon him?

John saw it, and by this he knew that Jesus was the Messiah; and therefore directed the people to Christ, saying, "Behold the Lamb of God, which taketh away the sin of the world." John 1 : 29 to 34.

How old was Jesus, when he was baptized?

About thirty years old.

Did John baptize any one after he baptized Jesus?

Yes; he baptized "in Enon near to Salim" at the same time the disciples of Jesus were baptizing in Judea. John 3: 22, 23, and 4 : 2,

What dispute arose about this time between some of John's disciples and the Jews? John 3 : 25.

A dispute in regard to purifying.

What do you suppose was the nature of that dispute?

I think it was because the disciples of John had neglected the Jewish rites of purifying since their baptism. (For some of those rites, read Numbers 19th ch.)

What did John say about this time in regard to his own mission and the mission of Christ?

He said, "He must increase, but I must decrease." John 3 : 30.

What did John say about faith in Christ?

"He that beleiveth on the Son hath everlasting life; and he that beleiveth not the Son shall not see life; but the wrath of God abideth on him." John 3: 36.

Do you believe on Christ as your personal Saviour?

How did John end his days?

He was put in prison by Herod because he reproved him for his wickedness, and was finally beheaded to satisfy the revenge of Herod's wife. Matt. 14: 3 to 12.

What two remarkable facts are seen in the life and death of John the Baptist?

He was the first preacher under the gospel dispensation, and the first martyr under that dispensation.

> Come, happy souls, adore the Lamb,
> Who loved our race ere time began,
> Who veiled his Godhead in our clay,
> And in an humble manger lay.
>
> To Jordan's stream the Spirit led,
> To mark the path his saints should tread
> With joy they trace the sacred way,
> To see the place where Jesus lay.
>
> Baptized by John in Jordan's wave,
> The Saviour left his watery grave;
> Heaven owned the deed, approved tho way,
> And blessed the place where Jesus lay.
>
> Come, all who love his precious name,
> Come, tread his steps, and learn of him;
> Happy beyond expression they
> Who find the place where Jesus lay.

LESSON X.

The Temptations of Christ.

Ques. What remarkable thing happened to Christ immediately after his baptism?

Ans. He was "led up of the Spirit into the wilderness to be tempted of the devil," where he fasted forty days and forty nights. Matt. 4: 1, 2.

How did the devil begin his temptations?

By saying to Christ, "if thou be the Son of God, command that these stones be made bread." Matt. 4: 3.

Is there any particular cunning in this temptation?

There is. Christ was hungry, and Satan embraced this as a favorable opportunity to induce him to yield to his temptations.

What argument did Satan use in this temptation?

"If thou be the Son of God;" in which Satan implies that if he did not turn the stones into bread to satisfy his hunger, that he could not be the Son of God.

How did Christ repulse the tempter in this temptation?

With the word of God; by saying, "It is written, Man shall not live by bread alone, but by every word that proceedeth out of the mouth of God." Matt. 4: 4.

What great truth is taught in this temptation?

That we should not yield to the temptations of Satan and commit sin because of present bodily necessities.

What was the next temptation?

"Then the devil taketh him into the holy city, and setteth him on a pinnacle of the temple, and saith unto him, If thou be the Son of God, cast thyself down; for it is written, He shall give his angels charge concerning thee; and in their hands they shall bear thee up, lest at any time thou dash thy foot against a stone." Matt. 4: 5, 6.

What was Christ's reply to this?

"It is written again, Thou shalt not tempt the Lord thy God." (v. 7) Here Christ asserts his divinity, and Satan is repulsed by the assertion.

What important lesson do we derive from this temptation?

That we should not rashly and unnecessarily expose our lives or persons to danger, and at the same time rely upon God to protect and sustain us.

What was the next temptation?

"Again the devil taketh him up into an exceeding high mountain, and showeth him all the kingdoms of the world, and the glory of them; and saith unto him, all these will I give thee, if thou wilt fall down and worship me." vs. 8, 9.

What was Christ's reply to this?

"Get thee hence, Satan; for it is written, thou shalt worship the Lord thy God, and him only shalt thou serve." v. 10.

What is particularly remarkable in this temptation?

That Satan rendered himself so contemptable by promising to give that which did not belong to him, and by presenting himself as a proper object of worship, that all that was necessary to repulse him was to *command* him to depart by authority of God's word.

What do we learn in these temptations in regard to the arguments to be employed against Satan and error?

We learn that they should be derived from the word of God.

What occurred immediately after these temptations?

"Then the devil leaveth him, and behold, angels came and ministered unto him." v. 11.

What may we expect if we properly resist the devil?

That he will flee from us, (James 4: 7,) and that we will enjoy the protection and consolation of God.

Why did Christ submit himself to the insolent temptations of Satan?

That in all things he might be made like unto his brethren, and that being tempted he might be able to succor them that are tempted. Heb. 2: 17, 18.

The Lord of glory moved by love,
Descends, in mercy, from above;
And he, before whom angels bow,
Is found a man of grief below.

Such love is great, too great for thought,
Its length and breadth in vain are sought,
No tongue can tell its depth and height;
The love of Christ is infinite.

But though his love no measure knows,
The Saviour to his people shows
Enough to give them joy, when known,
Enough to make their hearts his own.

LESSON XI.

The Ministry of Christ.

Ques. How did Christ commence his ministry?

Ans. By preaching the doctrine of repentance, saying as John had said, "Repent: for the kingdom of heaven is at hand."—Matt. 4 : 17.

Who were the first disciples of Christ?

Two of John's disciples. John 1 : 35—37.

What was the name of one of them?

Andrew, Simon Peter's brother. John 1: 40.

What did Andrew do soon after he became a disciple of Christ?

He found his brother Simon, and brought him to Jesus. John 1: 41, 42.

What practical lesson do we learn from the conduct of Andrew?

We learn that those who profess to be disciples of Christ should try to induce their friends and kindred to be his disciples also.

Why should they be particularly interested for the salvation of their friends and relatives? Ought they not to be interested for the salvation of all men?

It is true that they ought to have a general concern for the salvation of men; but they ought to labor *especially* for the salvation of their friends and relatives, because they are more likely to succeed with them in their private entreaties than they would be with strangers.

What did Christ say to Simon when he was brought to him by Andrew?

He said unto him, "Thou art Simon the son of Jonas: thou shalt be called Cephas, which is by interpretation, a stone." John 1 : 42.

How did Christ know the name of Simon and who his father was? did any one tell him?

I suppose not; but he knew them because he is God, and knows all things.

By what name is Simon usually called?

Peter.

Read Matt. 4 : 18—20, and tell me how the account there given of Peter and Andrew can be reconciled with the account given by John, which we have just examined.

The two are accounts of different transactions. John gives an account of Andrew and Peter becoming disciples, and Mathew of their call to the ministry.

Have we any account of any other of the first disciples bringing a friend to Christ?

Yes; we have a most interesting account of Philip's entreaties with Nathaniel. John 1 : 43—50.

Can you repeat this narative?
What is said of Christ's preaching, besides that he preached repentance?

That he preached the gospel of the kingdom. Matt. 4 : 23.

What practical lesson may be derived from what we have seen so far of the ministry of Christ?

That the proper way to make disciples of Christ is to teach men the gospel.

What is meant by being a disciple of Christ?

The same as being a christian.

Are you a disciple?

Doth Satan fill you with dismay,
And tell you, Christ will cast away;
It is a truth, why should you doubt?
He will in no wise cast you out.

Approach your God, make no delay,
He waits to welcome you to-day:
His mercy try, no longer doubt,
He will in nowise cast you out.

"Lord, at thy call, behold! I come
A guilty soul, lost and undone;
On thy rich blood I now rely,
O, pass my vile transgressions by."

LESSON XII.

Christ's Ministry.

Ques. When Christ made disciples, what was done to them?

Ans. They were baptized. John 3: 22, and 4: 1.

What does this fact teach us?

It teaches us that all christians should be baptized.

Did Christ make many disciples?

He made and baptized more disciples than John. John 4: 1.

Did Christ baptize any himself?

He did not, but his disciples did the baptizing under his authority. John 4: 2.

Who are authorized to baptize?

Those who have been baptized themselves, and have been set apart to the work of the gospel ministry. Matt. 28: 19.

Why do you say that a man must be baptized before he is authorized to baptize?

Because a man can not give that which he has not received.

But did not those baptisms of which we have been speaking, take place before any were chosen to the work of the ministry?

They did; but they were performed under the personal supervision of Christ, and by his direct authority.

Who baptized the first disciples of Christ?

John the Baptist.

Why do you say that they were baptized by John?

Because John's business was, "to make ready a people prepared for the Lord," (Luke 1 : 17,) and we have seen that the first disciples of Christ were those who had been John's disciples. John 1 : 35—37.

But were not those who had been baptized by John baptized over again?

There is no evidence that any of them were.

Whom did Christ choose as the first ministers of the gospel?

Twelve, whom he named apostles.

What were their names?

Peter, Andrew, James, John, Philip, Bartholomew, Matthew, Thomas, James, the son of Alpheus, Simon called Zelotes, Judas the brother of James, and Judas Iscariot.

Were all of these good men?

They were not; Judas Iscariot was a very bad man—so much so that Christ called him a devil. John 6 : 70.

What important lesson do we learn from this circumstance?

We learn not to judge of men from their position or office, but from their acts.

To whom did Christ send the twelve Apostles?

"To the lost sheep of the house of Israel." Matt. 10 : 6.

What does this mean?

It means that their labors were to be confined to the Jews, for they were specially commanded not to go to the Gentiles or to Samaritans. Matt. 10: 5..

What were they commanded to preach?

That "the kingdom of Heaven is at hand." Matt. 10: 7.

What does Mark say they preached?

"That men should repent." Mark 6: 12.

Was this according to their instructions?

It was; for the doctrine of repentance is an important doctrine of the kingdom.

What else did Christ tell them to do?

To "heal the sick, cleanse the lepers, raise the dead, and cast out devils." Matt. 6: 8.

Did they do any of these things?

"They cast out many devils, and anointed with oil many that were sick, and healed them." Mark 6: 13.

What did Christ tell the Apostles in regard to their support and providential protection?

"Provide neither gold nor silver, nor brass in your purses, nor scrip for your journey, neither two coats, neither shoes, nor yet staves; for the workman is worthy of his meat." Matt. 10: 10, 11.

What practical lesson is derived from this instruction?

That ministers of the gospel should be supported by those to whom they preach.

Did Christ choose any besides the twelve to the work of the ministry?

He did. He choose seventy others, and gave them similar authority to that of the twelve, and sent them out two and two. Luke 10th chapter.

When they returned to Christ what report did they bring?

They "returned with joy, saying, Lord, even the devils are subject unto us through thy name." Luke 10: 17.

What did Christ tell them in regard to their joy?

"In this rejoice not, because the spirits are subject unto you; but rather rejoice, because your names are written in heaven." Luke 10: 20.

What is better than all things else?

An assurance that our names are written in heaven.

Broad is the road that leads to death,
And thousands walk together there;
But wisdom shows a narrow path,
With here and there a traveller.

"Deny thyself and take thy cross,"
Is the Redeemer's great command:
Nature must count her gold but dross,
If she would gain this heavenly land.

Lord, let not all my hopes be vain,
Create my heart entirely new—
Which hypocrites could ne'er attain,
Which false apostates never knew.

LESSON XIII.

The Ministry of Christ.

Ques. Where did Christ commence his ministry?

Ans. In Galilee, the country where he lived.

What advantage does there seem to be in this?

If he had been a bad man, the people could have testified against him, for they knew him; but being a good man, nothing could be said against him.

How did he employ his time?

He "went about all Gallilee, teaching in their synagogues, and preaching the gospel of the kingdom, and healing all manner of sickness, and all manner of disease among the people." Matt. 4 : 23.

Did Christ continue to occupy his time in this way?

He did; for we have the same account in Matt 9 : 35.

What was the effect of these wonders which Christ performed?

"His fame went throughout all Syria; and they brought unto him all sick people that were taken with divers diseases and torments, and those, which were possessed with devils, and these which were lunatic, and those that had the palsy; and he healed them. And there followed him great multitudes of people from Galilee, and Decapolis, and Jerusalem, and Judea, and beyond Jordan." Matt. 4 : 24, 25.

Is it strange that such multitudes of people should follow him?

It is not, for the people of this country would act in the same way if such wonders were peformed among us.

After this what did Christ do?

He went up into a mountain, and called his disciples unto him, and taught them Matt. 5 : 1, 2.

Where are the teachings of Christ which he there delivered recorded?

In the 5th, 6th, and 7th chapters of Matt.

What are these teachings usually called?

Christ's sermon on the mount.

What is the character of Christ's teachings in this sermon?

He first tells us who are blessed, (ch. 5 : 3—11,) and then gives us important instructions for the regulation of our lives.

What does he tell his people they are?

That they are the salt of the earth, and the light of the world. ch. 5 : 13, 14.

What is the virtue of salt?

It is preserving, and so christians by their presence in the world preserve society from corruption and ruin.

What is the use of light?

That we may see surrounding objects,

and shun dangers, and follow after that which is good.

What does Christ tell his people to do, as the light of the world?

"Let your light so shine before men, that they may see your good works, and glorify your Father which is in heaven." v. 16.

What does he tell us about swearing?

"Swear not at all; but let your conversation be yea, yea,—nay, nay, for whatsoever is more than these cometh of evil." ch. 5 : 35—37.

What does he teach about resisting evil?

That we are not to resist evil, by rendering evil for evil, but to do good for evil. ch. 5 : 38—41.

What does he tell us in regard to our conduct toward our enemies?

"Love your enemies, bless them that curse you, do good to them that hate you, pray for them which despitefully use you and persecute you." ch 5 : 43—46.

If men generally would adopt this rule, what would be the effect?

The world would be much better off, and mankind much more happy.

    Compared with Christ, in all beside
      No comeliness I see;
    The one thing needful, dearest Lord,
      Is to be one with thee.

Less than thyself will not suffice
  My comforts to restore:
More than thyself I can not crave;
  Nor canst thou give me more.

Loved of my God, for him again
  With love intense I'd burn;
Chosen of thee, ere time began,
  I'd choose thee in return.

Whate'er consists not with thy will,
  O teach me to resign;
I'm rich to all th'intents of bliss,
  Since thou, my God, art mine.

LESSON XIV.

The Ministry of Christ.

Ques. What does Christ teach us about giving alms?

Ans. That we are not to give alms to be seen of men, for if we do we will have no reward of our heavenly Father. Matt. 6: 1—4.

What does he say of those who give alms that they may have glory of men?

He says that they are hypocrites, and that they have their reward.

What is the reward which such persons receive?

The reward that they seek, which is the praise of men.

What is the manner in which Christ tells his people that they must give alms?

That they must not let the left hand know what the right hand doeth.

What does this mean?

That they are to be quiet and unpretending in their charities, and bestow them alone for the sake of doing good.

If they do their alms thus secretly, what does Christ tell his people will be the effect?

"Thy Father which seeth in secret shall reward thee openly." v. 4.

Is it not better to have the reward which God bestows than to have the praise of men?

What does Christ teach in regard to prayer?

That we are not to pray as the hypocrites do, standing in the synagogues and in the corners of the streets, to be seen of men, but to pray to our heavenly Father in secret. vs. 5, 6.

What is a synagogue?

A house for Jewish worship.

What is a hypocrite?

One who pretends to be what he is not.

Are not hypocrites detestable characters?

They are; they are hateful both before God and man.

Do you suppose that Christ forbids all kinds of public prayer in this instruction?

I suppose not; but only that kind of public prayer practiced by the hypocrites.

What seemed to be the object of these hypocrites in their public prayers?

To be seen of men, and to be considered very holy.

Will it do us any good to be regarded by men as being very pious, if our hearts are not right in the sight of God?

It may do us some little good in this world, but it will be much worse for us in the world to come.

What farther instruction does Christ give in regard to prayer?

That we must not use vain repetitions, as the heathen do; for they think that they will be heard for their much speaking. v. 7.

From what we have seen, what does Christ seem to teach in regard to prayer?

That our prayers are to be simple, plain, and earnest.

Can you give any farther proof of this manner of prayer?

Christ teaches us to pray after this manner: "Our Father which art in heaven, hallowed be thy name. Thy kingdom come. Thy will be done in earth as it is in heaven. Give us this day our daily bread. And forgive us our debts, as we forgive our debtors. And lead us not into temptation, but deliver us from evil: for thine is the kingdom, and the power, and the glory forever." Amen. vs. 9—13.

What is this form of prayer usually called?

The Lord's prayer.

Is it necessary to use this particular form at all times?

I suppose not; but it is given to teach the *manner* of prayer.

What does Christ teach in regard to forgiveness?

"If ye forgive men their trespasses, your heavenly Father will also forgive you; but if ye forgive not men their trespasses, neither will your Father forgive your trespasses." vs. 14, 15.

Is it not a good thing to have the forgiveness of our heavenly Father?

> Our Father, God, who art in heaven,
> All hallowed be thy name;
> Thy kingdom come; thy will be done
> In heaven and earth the same.
>
> Give us this day our daily bread;
> And as we those forgive
> Who sin against us, so may we
> Forgiving grace receive.
>
> Into temptation lead us not;
> From evil set us free;
> And thine the kingdom, thine the power,
> And glory, ever be.

LESSON XV.

The Ministry of Christ.

Ques. What does Christ teach in regard to fasting?

Ans. That we should not fast, to appear unto men to fast, as the hypocrites do, but unto our heavenly Father. Matt. 6: 16, 17, 18.

What is a fast?

The fast which God has chosen is this: to loose the bands of wickedness, to undo the heavy burdens, to let the oppressed go free, to break every yoke, to feed the hungry, to bring the poor into your house, and to clothe the naked. Isaiah 58: 6, 7.

What is the ordinary signification of *fast?*

Acts of abstinence and humility.

How does this agree with what God describes as a fast which will be pleasing to him?

In this way: his people should abstain from personal interests and enjoyments, and humble themselves enough to do those things which he requires.

Where does Christ tell us to lay up our treasures?

In heaven, where moth and rust do not corrupt, and where theives do not break through and steal. Matt. 6: 20.

Where does he tell us our hearts will be?

Where our treasure is. Matt. 6: 21.

What is the christian's treasure which he lays up in heaven?

His hope of everlasting life.

How does he lay up this treasure?

By faith in Jesus Christ.

What does Christ teach in regard to serving God and mammon?

"Ye can not serve God and mammon." 24.

What is meant by mammon?

The word mammon is the name of the Syriac god of wealth: it means here, worldly possessions of all kinds.

What should be our first great care?

"Seek ye first the kingdom of God and his righteousness." v. 33.

What does Christ mean when he tells us to "take no thought" for various things necessary to our comfort in this life. v's 25--32?

I suppose he means to teach us that we are to discharge our various duties in the fear of God and not to be troubled about God's providential arrangements.

What does Christ teach in regard to judging one another?

"Judge not, that ye be not judged; for with what judgment ye judge, ye shall be judged; and with what measure ye mete, it shall be measured to you again." ch 7: 1, 2.

What is the meaning of this?

It seems to mean this: that we are not to form an unfavorable opinion of men before we know any thing about them; for after a while, by their fruits we can *know* them. v. 17.

What are we to understand in verses 3, 4, 5 by the mote and the beam in the eye?

We are here guarded against a captious spirit of magnifying the faults of others, while we may be doing much worse than they are.

What had we better do?

We had better correct our own faults first, and get rid of our sins, and then we will be much better prepared to assist others in reforming their lives.

What does Christ teach us about asking, seeking and knocking?

"Ask, and it shall be given you; seek, and ye shall find; knock, and it shall be opened unto you." v. 7.

For what are we to ask?

For the mercy of God, and the pardon of sin.

Will these be granted.

They will. v. 8.

For what are we to seek?

"For glory and honor and immortality." Rom. 2 : 7.

What will we find?

Eternal life. Rom. 2 : 7.

What may we understand by the expression "knock?"

We seem to be reminded here of the free and easy admittance which the children of God will have, when life's short journey is over, "into the everlasting kingdom of our Lord and Saviour Jesus Christ." 2 Peter 1 : 11.

Where will they then be?

In their Father's house. John 14 : 2.

There is a place of sacred rest,
 Far, far beyond the skies,
Where beauty smiles eternally,
 And pleasure never dies;—
My Father's house, my heavenly home,
 Where " many mansions" stand,
Prepared, by hands divine for all
 Who seek the better land.

In that pure home of tearless joy
 Earth's parted friends shall meet,
With smiles of love that never fade,
 And blessedness complete;
There, there adieus are sounds unknown;
 Death frowns not on that scene,
But life, and glorious beauty shine,
 Untroubled and serene.

LESSON XVI.

Ministry of Christ.

Ques. What is the character of those who will be admitted into the kingdom of heaven?

Ans. Christ says, "Not every one that saith unto me, Lord, Lord, ... but he that doeth the will of my Father which is in heaven." Matt. 7: 21.

What are we to understand by this?

That a mere profession of religion will not insure our admittance into heaven, but we must really and truly do the will of God.

What is the will of God?

It is that we believe in Jesus Christ, whom he hath sent into the world, and do whatsoever he has commanded. John 6 : 29, and 14 : 23, 24.

Where may we learn the commands of Christ?

In the New Testament.

Is it not an awful thing to make a false profession of religion?

It is; for, no matter how many wonders they perform in this world in the name of Christ, yet he will say unto them in the Judgment, "I never knew you : depart from me, ye that work iniquity." Matt. 7 : 22, 23.

What two gates does Christ tell us of in the 7th ch. of Matt.

The strait gate and the wide gate. 13th and 14th v's.

What is meant by "strait?"

Narrow or difficult.

To what way does this gate belong?

To the narrow way, which leadeth to life.

To what way does the wide gate belong?

To the broad way, which leadeth to destruction.

Which way has the greater number in it?

There are "many" in the broad way, and "few" in the narrow way.

In which way are you?

To what does Christ compare those who hear his sayings and do them?

To a wise man, which built his house upon a rock. v. 24.

What does he say of such a house.

"The rain descended, and the floods came and the winds blew, and beat upon that house; and it fell not: for it was founded upon a rock." v. 25.

What are we taught in this verse?

That genuine christians shall not be disappointed in their hope of heaven by even the most adverse outward circumstances.

Do christians build their hope of heaven upon a rock?

They do; upon the rock, Christ. 1 Peter 2 : 4.

Why is Christ compared to a rock?

Because of his firmness, stability and durability.

To what does Christ compare those who hear his sayings and do them not?

To a foolish man, who built his house upon the sand.

What does he say of such a house?

"The rain descended, and the floods came, and the winds blew, and beat upon that house, and it fell; and great was the fall of it." v. 27.

What do we learn from this?

That those who built their hope of heaven upon an improper foundation, will not be able to stand in the day of trial; and that the loss of the soul is great.

When the people had heard these wonderful teachings

of Christ in his sermon on the mount, how were they affected?

They " were astonished at his doctrine; for he taught them as one having authority, and not as the scribes." vs. 28, 29.

How should we be affected at the teachings of Christ?

We should believe, and obey them, because they are of divine authority, and are intended for our good.

> Strait is the way, the door is strait,
> That leads to joys on high:
> 'Tis but a few that find the gate,
> While crowds mistake and die.
>
> Beloved self must be denied,
> The mind and will renewed,
> Passion suppressed, and patience tried,
> And vain desires subdued.
>
> Lord, can a feeble, helpless worm
> Fulfill a task so hard?
> Thy grace must all the work perform,
> And give the free reward.

LESSON XVII.

Miracles of Christ.

Ques. When Christ had ended his sermon on the mount, and came down, who followed him?

Ans. Great multitudes followed him. Matt. 8:1.

Who came to Christ to be healed?

A leper.

What is a leper?

A person afflicted with the leprosy; which disease spreads itself entirely over the system, and is incurable by man.

Did Christ heal this leper?

He did. Matt. 8: 3.

What may we learn from this cure which Christ effected?

We learn these two things: 1st, The compassion of Christ for the afflicted; 2nd, His divinity; because he worked a miracle.

What may we *infer* from this cure?

That as Christ healed the leper who cried unto him, so he will heal our souls of the malady of sin if we cry unto him.

Was this the first miracle which Christ performed?

I suppose not: the first seems to have been performed in Cana of Galilee, when he turned the water into wine at the marriage. John, chap. 2.

What is a miracle?

It is a work not according to the ordinary operations of nature, and can be performed only by divine power.

Can you mention any others whom Christ healed?

He healed the centurion's servant without seeing him, and also Peter's wife's mother, and cast out many evil spirits, and healed many other sick people. Matt 8: 13—16.

What is a centurian?

A Roman officer who had charge of a hundred soldiers.

What remarkable miracle did Christ perform in the synagogue?

He commanded an unclean spirit to come out of a man, and he came out. Mark 1 : 26.

What did the man say when he saw Christ?

"He cried out, saying, Let us alone: what have we to do with thee, thou Jesus of Nazareth? art thou come to destroy us? I know thee who thou art, the Holy One of God." v. 24.

Whose language was this, the man's or the evil spirit's?

The words were spoken by the man, but he spoke them under the influence of the evil spirit.

To whom did Christ attribute the language?

To the spirit; for he commanded him to hold his peace, and to come out of the man. v. 25.

How were the people affected at this miracle?

They were greatly amazed, saying "what new thing is this? what new doctrine is this? for with authority he commandeth even the unclean spirits, and they do obey him." Mark 1 : 27.

What were these unclean spirits?

They were demons, which had taken wonderful possession of certain persons in those days.

Did Christ perform any other kind of miracle.

He did: he rebuked the wind, and subdued the tempest of the sea; and there was a great calm. Matt 8: 23—26.

How were those affected who saw this miracle?

They marveled and said, "what manner of man is this, that even the winds and the sea obey him." Matt. 8: 27, Mark 1: 27.

Why do you suppose the people were amazed at this miracle?

Because of an opinion held by the Jews that none but God could control the wind, but that many miracles connected immediately with the face of the earth could be performed by man.

With this opinion, what thought seemed natural to spring up in their minds, when they saw this miracle performed?

They thought that God was with them in human form.

Upon what sea was this miracle performed?

Perhaps it was the sea of Galilee.

Who met Christ when he crossed the sea and had gotten into the country of the Gergesenes?

There met him a wild man, possessed with a legion of devils, who had his dwelling among the tombs, and he was exceedingly fierce, or vicious, so that no man could pass that way. Matt. 8: 28—34, Mark 5: 1—17.

What did Christ do for this man?

He cast the devils out of him.

What became of the devils?

They went into a herd of swine, and the swine turned crazy, and ran down into the sea and were drowned.

What is said of the man?

He was found sitting, and clothed, and in his right mind."

After this great work had been done for this man, what did he desire?

He desired to be with Jesus. Mark 5 : 18.

What did Christ tell him?

He told him to go home to his friends, and tell them how great things the Lord had done for him. v. 19.

Did he obey Christ rather than follow his own inclination?

He did : " he departed, and began to publish in Decapolis how great things Jesus had done for him : and all men marveled." v. 20.

What may we learn from this fact?

We may learn two things: 1st, That when Christ has compassion on a sinner, and pardons his sins, it is right for him to make it known ; and 2nd, That at home among our friends is the place to begin.

And didst thou, Jesus, condescend
When veiled in human clay,
To heal the sick, the lame, the blind,
And drive disease away?

Didst thou regard the beggar's cry,
  And cause the blind to see?
Thou Son of David, hear—O, hear—
  Have mercy, too, on me.

And didst thou pity mortal woe,
  And sight and health restore?
O, pity, Lord, and save my soul,
  Which needs thy mercy more.

Didst thou thy trembling servant raise,
  When sinking in the wave?
I perish, Lord; O, save my soul;
  For thou alone canst save.

LESSON XVIII.

The Miracles of Christ.

Ques. When Christ passed over to the other side of the sea of Galilee, who met him?

Ans. A man named Jairus, who was a ruler of the synagogue. Mark 5: 20.

What did Jairus desire?

He besought Christ greatly that he would go and heal his little daughter, who lay at the point of death. v. 23.

How did Jairus approach Christ?

He fell down at his feet. v. 22.

What may we learn from this fact?

We may learn two things, namely: 1st, That Jairus was deeply in earnest; 2nd, That it is proper to approach Christ in great humility.

Did Christ regard the prayer of Jairus?

He did; and went with him.

What report was brought to Jairus while he was on his way home with Christ?

That his daughter was dead. v. 35.

What did Christ say to Jairus?

"Be not afraid, only believe." v. 36.

What did Christ then do?

He went on to the house of Jairus.

When he arrived at the house what did he say?

"Why make ye this ado, and weep? the damsel is not dead, but sleepeth." v. 39.

Did those who heard these words receive them as words of mercy and grace?

They did not, but they regarded them as words of folly, for "they laughed him to scorn." v. 40.

Do not many now regard the gracious words of Christ in the same light?

They do; and it is folly and shame in them so to do.

What did Christ then do?

He went into the room where the dead child was lying, with her father and mother, and took her by the hand, and said unto her, "Damsel, arise," and she immediately arose, and walked. v's 40—42.

How old was this little girl?

About twelve years old.

What consoling thought may we derive from this narative?

That when Christ is engaged in a work of mercy and grace, he is not turned aside from its performance by the scoffs and jeers of unbelievers.

What remarkable occurence took place while Christ was on his way to th house of Jarius?

A woman who was greatly diseased, and could not be cured by the physicians, went up behind Christ, in the great crowd, and touched his garment and was immediately cured. v's 25—34.

What did this woman say about this matter?

She said, "If I may but touch his clothes, I shall be whole." v. 28.

What does this saying of the woman show?

It shows that she had great faith.

What did Christ say after the woman had touched his clothes?

He said, "Who touched my clothes?" v. 30.

Why did he ask this question?

Because he felt that virtue had gone out of him. v. 30.

What reply did his disciples make to his question?

They said unto him, "Thou seest the multitude thronging thee, and sayest thou, who touched me?"

When Jesus looked around, what affecting sight was seen?

"The woman fearing and trembling, knowing what was done in her, came and fell down before him, and told him all the truth." v. 33.

What did Christ then say to her?

"Daughter thy faith hath made thee whole; go in peace, and be whole of thy plague." v. 34.

What important religious truth do we derive from the narrative?

The great power of faith in Christ, to secure to us the blessings we need.

What did she desire?

Faith is a precious grace,
  Where'er it is bestowed;
It boasts a high, celestial birth,
  And is the gift of God.

Jesus it owns as King,
  And all-atoning Priest;
It claims no merit of its own,
  But looks for all in Christ

To him it leads the soul,
  When filled with deep distress,
Flies to the fountain of his blood,
  And trusts his righteousness.

Since 'tis thy work alone,
  And that divinely free,
Lord, send the Spirit of thy Son,
  To work this faith in me.

LESSON XIX.

The Miracles of Christ.

Ques. When Christ was in the coast of Tyre and Sidon, who came to him? Matt. 15: 21—28.

Ans. A woman of Canaan, of the same coast, who was a gentile.

What did she desire?

That he would heal her daughter, who was grievously vexed with a devil.

Did he immediately grant her request?

He did not: "he answered her not a word." v. 23.

What did his deciples desire him to do?

They requested him to send her away.

Why did they make this request?

Because they felt disturbed by her incessant cries; for they said, "she crieth after us." v. 23.

What did Christ then say?

He said, "I am not come but unto the lost sheep of the house of Israel." v. 24.

What encouragement may be derived from this saying of Christ?

That he is the friend of lost sinners, especially of those who truly feel their condition.

How did it affect the woman?

"Then she came and worshiped him saying, Lord, help me." v. 25.

What did Christ then say to her?

"It is not meet to take the children's bread and to cast it to dogs." v. 26.

What is meant by this?

By "children" is meant the Jews, by "dogs" is meant the Gentiles, and by "bread" is meant the blessings which Christ had to bestow.

What does all this put together seem to teach?

That it was not according to regular order to offer the blessings of the gospel to the Gentiles, until a full offer had been made to the Jews.

Why did Christ, who was all goodness, use such a low term as "dog" to designate the Gentiles?

This being a term of reproach used by the Jews in regard to the Gentiles, he used it, no doubt, to test her faith and humanity.

What was the woman's reply to Christ?

"Truth Lord; yet the dogs eat of the crumbs which fall from their master's table."

What did she mean by this answer?

She meant, no doubt, that when the Jews were well supplied, she was willing to take the meanest portion of the benefits of Christ.

And must not every one who approaches Christ possess a similar spirit to this?

He must. He must be willing to have just what Christ will give, to receive any thing at all.

What did Christ finally say to the woman? and what happened to her daughter?

He said unto her, "woman, great is thy faith: be it unto thee even as thou wilt. And her daughter was made whole from that very hour." v. 28.

After this where did Christ go? and who came unto him?

He went up on a mountain near the sea of Galilee, and a great multitude came unto him, bringing with them the lame, the blind, the dumb, the maimed, and many others; and cast them down at Jesus' feet; and he healed them. v's 29, 30.

How were the people affected when they saw these wonderful miracles?

They "wondered, when they saw the dumb to speak, the maimed to be whole, the lame to walk, and blind to see: and they glorified the God of Israel." v. 31.

How should we be affected when we see Christ's wonderful works of mercy and grace to mankind?

We should also glorify the God of Israel.

Christ was now in the wilderness, with four thousand people around him, and they were hungry, and had no bread but seven loaves, and a few little fishes—what did he do?

He blessed that bread and the fishes, and broke them, and fed the whole multitude; and when they had all eaten they had more left than they had at the beginning; for they took up of what remained seven baskets Matt. 15: 32—38.

How was this?

It was a great miracle. The bread and the fishes, under the blessing of Christ, greatly multiplied.

What may we learn from this remarkable miracle?

That Christ can supply our greatest wants, under the most pressing circumstances.

A friend there is—your voices join,
  Ye saints, to praise his name—
Whose truth and kindness are divine,
  Whose love's a constant flame.

When most we need his gracious hand,
  This friend is always near;
With heaven and earth at his command,
  He waits to answer prayer.

His love no end or measure knows,
  No change can turn its course;
Immutably the same it flows
  From one eternal source.

LESSON XX.

The Miracles of Christ.

Ques. Did Christ feed any others by miracle besides the four thousand of which we spake in the preceeding lesson?

Ans. He did. He fed five thousand on another occasion, in a similar way. Mark 6: 33—44.

How many loaves and fishes had he to begin with on this occasion?

Five loaves and two fishes.

How many baskets full of the fragments were taken up on this occasion?

Twelve.

After this miracle, where did Jesus send his disciples?

He sent them by ship to the other side of the lake of Gennesareth. Mark 6: 45.

What kind of a place was Gennesareth?

It was a city, situate at the north end of lake Gennesareth just where the river Jordan flows into the lake.

Where did Christ then go?

He went up on a mountain to pray. v. 46.

What does this circumstance teach us?

It teaches us the great importance of prayer.

What kind of voyage had the disciples in crossing the lake?

They had rather a hard voyage; for the wind was contrary, and they had to toil much in rowing. v. 48.

While thus toiling in the ship, what did they see?

They saw Jesus walking on the sea, and thought that it was a spirit, and were afraid until he spake unto them. v's 48, 49.

What did he say to them?

"Be of good cheer: it is I; be not afraid." v. 50.

What happened when Christ went into the ship?

The wind ceased. v. 51.

Did you ever know a man to walk on the water? What consoling thought may be derived from this circumstance?

That Christ is often near his people in times of trouble and danger, to protect and comfort them, when they are least thinking of his presence.

What wonderful things happened when Christ had gotten over into the land of Gennesareth?

Wherever he went, into villages, or cities, or country, the people laid the sick in the streets, and besought him that they might touch but the border of his garment; and as many as touched him were made whole. v 56, Matt. 14: 36.

What remarkable miracle did Christ perform in Bethsaida? Mark 8: 22—26.

He restored a blind man to his sight, by spitting on his eyes, and laying his hands on him.

Did this man see clearly at first?

He did not; for he said that he saw men as trees walking.

What did Christ then do to him?

He laid his hands on his eyes again; and he was restored, and saw every man clearly.

What may we learn from this miracle?

That Christ will not leave a work half

done which he undertakes, but will complete it.

There is another remarkable account of a blind man being restored to sight by Christ—can you tell me where it is, and something about it?

It is recorded in the 9th chapter of John. The man was born blind; Christ spit on the ground and made clay and anointed the eyes of the man with it; sent him to the pool of Siloam to wash his eyes; he went and washed, and returned *seeing*.

Where was the pool of Siloam?

It was near the eastern wall of the temple in Jerusalem.

What took place among the Pharisees in consequence of this miracle?

A controversy in regard to Christ. Some said he was not of God, and others said, "how can a man that is a sinner do such miracles?"

What did the man who had been blind say of Christ?

He said "He is a prophet."

What did the Jews do in this matter?

They held a long controversy with the man in regard to Christ; and when the man manifested great attachment for Christ, they cast him out from their society.

Who met the man after this?

Jesus met him, and comforted him; and revealed himself to him as the Messiah;

and the man believed in him, and worshipped him.

Ought not all of us to believe in Jesus, and worship him?

One there is, above all others,
  Well deserves the name of Friend!
His is love beyond a brother's,
  Costly, free, and knows no end.

Which of all our friends, to save us,
  Could or would have shed his blood?
But this Saviour died to have us
  Reconciled in him to God.

When he lived on earth abased,
  Friend of sinners was his name;
Now, above all glory raised,
  He rejoices in the same.

O! for grace our hearts to soften;
  Teach us, Lord, at length to love;
We, alas! forget too often
  What a friend we have above.

LESSON XXI.

The Miracles of Christ.

Ques. What notable miracle did Jesus perform near the city of Nain? Luke 7: 11—18.

He restored to life a young man who was being carried to his burial.

Whose son was this young man?

He was the only son of a widow. v. 12.

Were there many people accompanying the corpse to the grave?

There were. v. 12.

What inference may be drawn from this fact?

That the young man and his mother were persons of some distinction.

What influence would this fact have on the miracle?

It would give it greater currency in the community, and place the fact of its performance beyond the power of contradiction.

How was Jesus exercised towards the mother of the young man when he saw her?

"He had compassion on her, and said unto her, weep not." v. 13.

What did he then do?

"He came and touched the bier; and they that bare stood still. And he said, young man, I say unto thee arise. And he that was dead sat up, and began to speak. And he delivered him to his mother." verses 14, 15.

What did the people say about Christ?

They said, "that a great prophet is risen up among us; and, that God hath visited his people." v. 16.

Did Christ raise any one else from the dead?

He did; he raised up Lazarus, after he had been dead four days, and was buried. John, chap. 11.

Where did Lazarus live?

In the town of Bethany.

Who were his sisters?

Martha and Mary.

What did Martha say to Christ when he told her that her brother should rise again?

She said, "I know that he shall rise again in the resurrection at that last day." v. 24.

What did Jesus then say to her?

He said, "I am the resurrection, and the life: he that believeth in me, though he were dead, yet shall he live." v. 25.

How was Jesus affected when he saw the great distress occasioned by the death of Lazarus?

"Jesus wept." v. 35.

What may we learn from this fact?

That Jesus has a deep sympathy for the distresses and sufferings of his people.

What did the Jews say when they saw Jesus weeping?

They said, "Behold how he loved him."

When Jesus came to the grave of Lazarus, what did he do to raise him from the dead?

"He cried with a loud voice, Lazarus, come forth."

What then happened?

"And he that was dead came forth, bound hand and foot with grave clothes; and his face was bound about with a napkin."

Is not the time coming when all the dead will be raised at the bidding of Christ?

It is; "for the hour is coming, in the which all that are in the graves shall hear his voice, and shall come forth; they that have done good, unto the resurrection of life: and they that have done evil, unto the resurrection of damnation." John 5: 28, 29.

Can you now name the several kinds of miracles which Christ performed?

He turned water into wine, he cleansed the lepers, he gave sight to the blind and hearing to the deaf, he caused the dumb to speak and the lame to walk, he restored the maimed to soundness and healed all manner of diseases, he fed the hungry and stilled the raging of the sea, he cast out devils and raised the dead.

What must we say of one who can perform such miracles as these?

That he is God manifest in the flesh, and is altogether worthy of our adoration and worship.

Jesus, my Lord, I own thee God,
Earth sprang to being at thy nod;
All things were made by thee, the Word,
Who wast, with God, as God adored.

Before the world's firm base was laid,
Thy glorious Godhead was displayed;
And after worlds have ceased to be,
Thy praise shall fill eternity.

Thou, gracious Lord, my soul would own,
The power to save is thine alone;
O'er me assert thy sovereign will,
And be my God, my Saviour still.

LESSON XXII.

The Teachings of Christ.

Ques. How did Christ mostly teach?

Ans. By parables.

What is a parable?

It is to compare, or to place side by side. In the parables of Christ he compares natural things with spiritual things.

What is the first parable of our Lord's which is recorded?

The parable of the sower. Matt. 12. Mark 4, Luke 8.

On how many sorts of ground did the seed fall?

Some fell by the way-side; some on stony ground; some among thorns; and some on good ground.

What became of that which fell by the wayside?

The fowls of the air devoured it.

What does this represent?

It represents those who hear the word of God, and "Satan cometh immediately, and taketh away the word that was sown in their hearts."

What became of the seed that was sown on stony ground?

It immediately sprung up, because it had no depth of earth; but when the sun was up, it was scorched; and because it had no root, it withered away."

What class of persons does this represent?

Those who received the word with gladness, but have no root in themselves, and endure for a while, but fall away in times of persecution. v's 16, 17.

What is meant by "have no root in themselves?"

It means, no doubt, that religion is not truly fixed in their hearts.

What became of the seed that was sown among thorns?

It grew up, and was choked, and yielded no fruit.

What class of persons does this represent?

"Such as hear the word, and the cares of this world, and the deceitfulness of riches, and the lusts of other things entering in, choke the word, and it becometh unfruitful."

What became of the seed that was sown on good ground?

It grew up, and increased, and yielded fruit; some thirty, some sixty and some an hundred fold.

What class of persons does this represent?

It represents genuine christians, who bear the fruits of holiness—some thirty, some sixty and some an hundred fold—and in the end have everlasting life. v. 20. Rom. 6: 22.

Who does the sower in the parable represent?

It represents Christ.

How is Christ now sowing the word?

By his ministers, and all others of his people who are engaged in spreading religious truth in the world.

What parable, similar to the one already considered, did Christ give us, illustrative of the kingdom of heaven?

The parable of the good seed and the tares. Matt. 13 : 24—30.

Who sowed the good seed?

Christ. Matt. 13 : 37.

Who sowed the tares?

Satan or the devil. Matt. 13 : 29.

What is the field in which these seeds are sown?

The world.

Who are the good seed?

The children of the kingdom. v. 38.

Who are the tares?

The children of the wicked one. v. 38.

What is the harvest?

The end of the world. v. 39.

Who are the reapers?

The angels. v. 39.

What is to be done with the tares, or the offenders against God, in this great harvest?

They shall be cast into a furnace of fire, where there shall be wailing and gnashing of teeth. v. 42.

What will become of the good seed, or the righteous?

They shall shine forth as the sun in the kingdom of their Father. v. 43.

In which company do you hope to be?

This is the field, the world below,
Where wheat and tares together grow;
Where oft we see, in mingled band,
Sinners and saints together stand ;
  But soon the reaping-time will come,
  And angels shout the harvest home.

We seem as one, when thus we meet,
And bow before the mercy-seat ;
But to the Lord's all-searching eyes,
Each heart appears without disguise :
  And soon the reaping-time, &c.

To love my sins, a saint t' appear,
To grow with wheat, and be a tare,
May serve me while on earth below,
Where tares and wheat together grow ;
  But soon the reaping-time, &c.

Most awful truth! And is it so ?
Must all mankind the harvest know ?
Is every one a wheat or tare ?
Me for the harvest, Lord, prepare ;
  For soon the reaping-time, &c.

Then all who truly righteous are,
Shall in their Father's Kingdom share,
But tares in bundles shall be bound,
And cast in hell. O, doleful sound !
  And soon the reaping-time will come,
  And angels shout the harvest home.

LESSON XXIII.

The Teachings of Christ.

Ques. Can you mention any other parables of Christ illustrative of his kingdom ?

Ans. I can : the parable of the mustard

seed,—the parable of the leaven,—the parable of the treasure in the field,—the parable of the merchant, and the parable of the net. Matt. 13.

How do these different parables represent one and the same kingdom?

They represent different things belonging to that kingdom.

In the parable of the mustard seed, Matt. 13: 31, 32, what does the little mustard seed represent?

It represents the word of divine truth, which is very small in the estimation of wicked men, and that the beginning of christianity in the world is small.

What does the sowing of this seed in the field represent?

It represents the fact that God has sent down his truth into this wicked world.

What does the growing up of this little seed into a great herb represent?

It represents the great increase and extension of Christ's kingdom in the world.

What does the lodging of birds in the branches of this great herb represent?

It represents that those who are so disposed by divine grace, can find a lodgement in the kingdom of Christ, where they may rest from their weary wanderings.

What does the parable of the leaven represent? Mat. 13: 33.

This represents, most fitly, the influ-

which the grace of God has upon our entire life, when it is deposited in our hearts. It continues to extend its influence, until our whole life is brought under the authority of Christ.

Can you explain the parable of the treasure hid in the field, which a man found, and then sold all he had to buy that field? Matt. 13: 44.

This teaches us, that when a man has found the true religion of Christ, that he will give up every other religious notion for it.

What does the parable of the merchantman represent? verses 45, 46.

This seems to represent the same thing as the other.

What is the difference between the religion of Christ and all other religions?

The religion of Christ is true; it came from heaven, and leads to heaven; all other religion is false, and leads to perdition.

What do we learn from the parable of the net? verses 47, 48.

We learn that there are in the church both good and bad.

When are the good and the bad to be separated?

At the end of the world. v. 49.

By whom is the separation to be made?

By the angels. v. 49.

What will become of the good?

They will be saved. v. 48.

What will become of the wicked?

They will be cast away into a furnace of fire. v. 50.

What do we learn from this solemn declaration of our Lord?

We learn that the mere fact of a man's being a member of the church will do him no good at the judgement day, if he is a wicked man; that then, all wicked men will share the same fate, whether they are members of the church or not. Compare verses 42 and 50.

Is this solemn truth taught any where else in the New Testament?

It is, Luke 13: 26, 27--"Then shall ye begin to say, we have eaten and drunk in thy presence, and thou hast taught in our streets. But he shall say, I tell you, I know you not whence ye are; depart from me all ye workers of iniquity."

What practical influence should these solemn truths have on our lives?

We should constantly examine ourselves, to see if we are in the faith, and pray earnestly unto God to suffer us not to be deceived in our religion.

When thou, my righteous Judge, shall come
To take thy ransomed people home,
 Shall I among them stand?
Shall such a worthless worm as I,
Who sometimes am afraid to die,
 Be found at thy right hand?

I love to meet thy people now,
Before thy feet with them to bow,
  Though vilest of them all ;
But—can I bear the piercing thought?—
What if my name should be left out,
  When thou for them shalt call ?

O Lord, prevent it by thy grace ;
Be thou my only hiding-place,
  In this th' accepted day ;
Thy pardoning voice, O, let me hear,
To still my unbelieving fear,
  Nor let me fall, I pray.

And when the final trump shall sound,
Among thy saints let me be found,
  To bow before thy face :
Then in triumphant strains I'll sing,
While heaven's resounding mansions ring
  With praise of sovereign grace.

LESSON XXIV.

The Manner of Christ's Living.

Ques. In what manner did Christ live?

Ans. He lived as a poor man. He said of himself: "The foxes have holes, and the birds of the air have nests; but the Son of man hath not where to lay his head." Matt. 8 : 20.

What effect did the humble circumstances of Christ have upon some who heard him?

They contemned him, and said, " Is not this the carpenter, the son of Mary, the brother of James, and Joses, and of Juda and Simon? and are not his sisters here with us?" Mark 6 : 3.

Where did this take place?

In Galilee, his own country. v. 1.

Did not Christ teach with great wisdom on this occasion?

He did: insomuch that the people were greatly astonished that he possessed such wisdom. v. 2.

What may we learn from the poverty of Christ, and the manner in which he was treated on account of his poverty?

1st. That the greatest religious wisdom is often found in the humbler walks of life. 2nd. That men generally are influenced too much by external circumstances, in religion, for God's truth is the same, whether spoken by the rich or the poor.

Did Christ choose to be poor in this world, rather than rich?

He did; for he was God, as well as man, and acted in this matter according to his sovereign pleasure.

Why did Christ choose a life of poverty while on earth?

That he might be in nearer sympathy with the largest number of people, and that the truth of his doctrine might be proved, when he said, "my kingdom is not of this world."

But could he not have been in equal sympathy with the poor if he had been rich?

It is true, as God, he could, but the poor themselves would not have so regarded him; for, as a general rule, the rich have but little sympathy for the poor.

What other evidence does Christ give of his sympathy for the poor?

He preached the gospel unto them, and mingled with them. Matt. 11 : 5.

What class of people gave most attention to the teachings of Christ?

"The common people heard him gladly." Mark 12 : 37.

What good reason can be assigned for this fact?

Christ's manner of life, and his mode of teaching, were both adapted to this class of people.

What practical lesson may be derived from Christ's manner of life?

We learn that those ministers of the gospel who would follow Christ closely, and be wise in winning souls to him, must adapt their manner of life to the circumstances of those for whom they labor.

Can you give an example of any of the early preachers of the gospel acting in this way?

Paul, speaking of his manner of life as a minister of the Gospel, says: "I am made all things to all men, that I might by all means save some." 1 Cor. 9 : 22.

Did Christ do any thing wrong?

He did no sin, neither was guile found in his mouth. 1 Peter 2 : 22.

Did he mingle with sinners?

He did; and also ate with them. Matt. 9 : 11.

What was Christ called on this account?

He was called, by way of reproach, "a friend of publicans and sinners." Matt. 11 : 19.

Is it any reproach to Christ that he was a friend of sinners?

It is not; but it will be the crown of rejoicing by redeemed sinners for ever. Rev. 1 : 5, 6.

What may be said of the manner of Christ's life, specially claiming our imitation?

He was often engaged in prayer.

"Cold mountains and the midnight air
Witnessed the fervor of his prayer."

LESSON XXV.

Christ rejected by the Jews.

Ques. Were the people who heard the teachings of Christ and saw his miracles friendly toward him?

Ans. They were not; for many hated him with cruel hatred, and persecuted him.

Who were the leaders in opposition to Christ?

The Scribes and Pharisees.

Who were the Scribes and Pharisees?

The Scribes were those who were learned in the Jewish law. The Pharisees were a set of Jews who separated themselves from the other Jews, as well as from the Gentiles, under pretenses of great holiness.

What did Christ teach his people in regard to the righteousness necessary for them to possess?

"Except your righteousness shall exceed *that* of the Scribes and Pharisees, ye shall in no case enter into the kingdom of heaven." Matt. 5 : 20.

To what righteousness does our Lord here refer, as necessary for his people?

It is, no doubt, the same spoken of by Paul—that which is not of the law, "but that which is through the faith of Christ, the righteousness which is of God by faith." Phil. 3 :. 9.

What is this righteousness called by theologians?

It is called, the imputed righteousness of Christ.

What is meant by "the imputed righteousness of Christ"?

It means that when we exercise true faith in Christ, his righteousness is placed to our account, and we have the same benefit of it as if we had performed it ourselves.

What was the righteousness of the Scribes and Pharisees?

It was their own righteousness.

What is said of this kind of righteousness. Isaiah 64 : 6.

It is called filthy rags; which signifies

that it is like a badly torn and filthy garment, which would render us unfit for decent company.

What did Christ call the Scribes and Pharisees?

He called them hypocrites, and fools, and pronounced terrible woes against them. Matt. 23 : 13—19.

Did not these people perform many outward religious acts?

They did, see Matt. 23 : 1—7.

What may we learn from this?

That no outward religious services will avail us any thing if our hearts are not right in the sight of God.

What was the probable cause of the Scribes and Pharisees' hatred of Christ?

It was, no doubt, on account of his frequent exposure of their hypocracy.

Did any others, besides the Scribes and Pharisees, hate Christ?

They did. The most of the Jews hated him, and spoke evil of him, and persecuted him.

What did they say of him?

They said that he was a gluttonous man, and a wine-bibber, Matt. 11 : 19—that he was a blasphemer, Matt. 9 : 3—John 10 : 33—that he was a Sabbath breaker, John 9 : 16—and that he had a devil. John 7 : 20, 8 : 48, 52, and 10 : 20.

Why did they say that he had a devil?

Because he accused them of their wickedness in going about to kill him, and declared that he was the Son of God. John 7: 19, 10: 7—21.

Did the Jews attempt any personal violence against Christ?

They did. On one occasion they attempted to cast him headlong over the brow of the hill on which the city of Nazarath was built, (Luke 4: 29,) and on several occasions took up stones to cast at him. John 8: 39, 10: 31.

What does John say of the rejection of Christ by the Jews?

He says: "He came unto his own, and his own received him not." John 1: 11.

How was Christ affected towards the Jews when they had given such repeated evidence of their rejection and hatred of him?

On one occasion he said, "O Jerusalem, Jerusalem, which killest the prophets and stonest them that are sent unto thee; how often would I have gathered thy children together, as a hen doth gather her brood under her wings, and ye would not: behold your house is left unto you desolate." Luke 12: 34, 35. And on another occasion, when he beheld the city, he wept over it. Luke 19: 41.

What is meant by the expresssion, "Your house is left unto you desolate"?

It means that God had forsaken them.

What do we learn from the conduct of Christ towards the Jews after such evidences which he had of their rejection and hatred of him?

We learn the tenderness of his heart even towards his worst enemies.

What national calamities came upon the Jews on account of their rejection of Christ?

Their city (Jerusalem) and their beautiful temple were destroyed by the Romans, and they have been dispersed among all nations of the earth, even to this very time.

What will be our doom if we reject Christ?

We will be rejected by him in the great Judgment day.

 Did Christ o'er sinners weep,
  And shall our cheeks be dry?
 Let floods of penitential grief
  Burst forth from every eye.

 The Son of God in tears
  The wondering angels see;
 Be thou astonished, O my soul!
  He shed those tears for thee.

 He wept that we might weep;
  Each sin demands a tear;
 In heaven alone no sin is found,
  And there's no weeping there.

LESSON XXVI.

Sufferings of Christ.

Ques.—At what time did the sufferings and death of Christ take place?

Ans. At the feast of the Passover.

What is meant by the feast of the Passover?

It was a feast of seven days continuance, kept by the Jews in memory of their deliverance from Egypt. Exodus, chap. 12.

Did Christ keep this feast?

He did. He kept it with his disciples in an upper room in the city of Jerusalem, Mark 14: 10—18.

What memorable thing did Jesus do at this feast?

He instituted what is called the Lord's Supper. Matt. 26: 26—30, Mark 14: 22—25, Luke 22: 19, 20.

Where did Christ and his disciples go after supper was over?

They went to the mount of Olives.

Where was Christ next seen?

At Gethsemane, in great agony and in earnest prayer. Matt. 26: 36—45.

What did Christ say to his disciples on this occasion?

He said unto them, "My soul is exceeding sorrowful, even unto death."

What does Luke say of the manner in which Christ was affected on this occasion?

"And being in an agony, he prayed

more earnestly: and his sweat was as it were great drops of blood falling down to the ground." ch. 22: 44.

Did you ever see or hear of such intense suffering as this in any one besides Christ?

Why were his sufferings so great, was he afraid of death?

He was not afraid of death, because he had frequently declared that he would rise from the dead.

Why then was he so agonized?

Because the Lord had laid our sins upon him, and he was then bearing them in his own person, that he might cancel them by offering up himself as an everlasting sacrifice unto God. Isaiah, 53rd chapter, Heb. 9: 14.

Who appeared unto Christ while he was in his great agony?

An angel from heaven appeared unto him, strengthening him. Luke 22: 43.

Who came unto him after this?

Judas, with a great multitude with swords and staves from the chief priests and elders of the people. Matt. 26: 47.

Who betrayed Christ?

Judas betrayed him with a kiss. v. 49.

Where did these wicked people take Christ?

They took him first to Caiaphas, the high priest, where they brought false witness against him, and spit upon him, and smote him with rods. Matt. 26: 60—67.

Where did they take him the next morning?

They took him to Pontius Pilot, the governor. Matt. 27: 1.

What did Pilot ask the Jews?

He asked them whom he should release unto them, Jesus, or Barabbus.

Whom did they prefer?

They chose Barabbus, who was a murderer. Luke 23: 19.

What did the Jews say must be done with Christ?

They said let him be crucified. v. 22.

What did Pilot do with Jesus?

He sent him to Herod, who at that time was in Jerusalem. Luke 23: 7.

How did Herod treat him?

He set him at nought, and mocked him, and arrayed him in a gorgeous robe, and sent him again to Pilot. Luke 23: 11.

After Pilot had heard all that the Jews had to say against Christ, was he willing to release him?

He was, but the Jews cried "crucify him, crucify him." Luke 23: 21.

Did Pilot find any cause of death in Christ?

He did not; but the voices of Christ's enemies prevailed over his judgement, and he delivered Christ into their hands. Luke 23: 22—24.

Ought men to do wrong to please the multitude?

They ought not, but they should do right at all times, and under all circumstances.

>Dark was the night and cold the ground
>   On which the Lord was laid ;
>His sweat like drops of blood ran down ;
>   In agony he prayed :
>
>"Father remove this bitter cup,
>   If such thy sacred will ;
>If not, content to drink it up,
>   Thy pleasure I fulfil."
>
>Go to the garden, sinner: see
>   Those precious drops that flow ;
>The heavy load he bore for thee ;
>   For thee he lies so low.
>
>Then learn of him the cross to bear;
>   Thy fathers will obey :
>And when temptations press the near.
>   Awake to watch and pray.

LESSON XXVII.

Christ Crucified.

Ques. Where was Christ crucified?

Ans. At the place called Calvary and Golgotha, which latter name signifies "a place of a skull." Matt. 27: 33.

Where is Calvary situated?

A short distance west of Jerusalem.

At what time in the day was Christ crucified?

It was the third hour of the day, which

corresponds to nine o'clock according to our time. Mark 15: 25.

What is meant by being crucified?

It was the Roman method of executing those who were condemned to die.

What is the manner of crucifying?

There was a long beam of wood prepared with a cross beam near the top end.. This made the cross. It was laid on the ground, and the person to be crucified was laid on it with his back next to the wood. His arms were then extended on each side, and his hands nailed to the cross beam; and his feet were extended on the long beam and nailed to it. Then the cross, with the person so fastened to it, was lifted up in an upright position, and the foot of it placed in a hole in the earth prepared to receive it.

Who carried the cross on which Christ was crucified?

He first bore it himself and afterwards it was borne by one Simon of Cyrene. John 19: 17. Matt. 27: 32.

What did Christ do when he was crucified?

He prayed for his persecutors, "Father forgive them, for they know not what they do." Luke 23 : 34.

What dreadful exclamation did he make while on the cross?

He cried with a loud voice, "My God,

my God, why hast thou forsaken me?"— Matt. 27: 46.

Did he say anything more than this on the cross?

He did. He said, "It is finished," and "Father, into thy hands I commend my spirit." (John 19: 30, Luke 23: 46,) and then bowed his head and gave up the ghost.

What was the superscription Pilot wrote for Christ?

"THIS IS THE KING OF THE JEWS." Luke 23: 38.

What is meant by superscription?

It was a writing placed over the person who was crucified to show who he was.

In how many languages was the superscription which was placed over Christ written?

In three—Greek, Latin, and Hebrew. Luke 23: 88.

Why was it written in these three languages?

So that all present could read it, for there were persons present who spake and read these different languages.

Were the Jews satisfied with this superscription?

They were not; but wanted Pilot to write, "He said, ' I am king of the Jews.' " John 19: 21.

What was Pilot's reply to this request of the Jews?

Pilot answered, "What I have written, I have written." John 19: 22.

How long did Christ hang upon the cross before he died?

From the third to the sixth hour, (Mark 15 : 33,) making three hours.

What remarkable thing occurred at this time?

There was darkness over all the land from the sixth to the ninth hour. Luke 23 : 44.

Was this darkness noticed by any other people except those of Judea?

It is said to have been noticed by the Egyptian philosophers, and that they said, "Surely the God of nature must be suffering."

Who were crucified with Christ?

Two malefactors, who were thieves, and condemned to die for their wickedness.—Matt. 27 : 44, Luke 23 : 39.

What did these thieves do?

One railed on Christ, and the other prayed, "Lord, remember me when thou comest into thy kingdom." Luke 23 : 39—42.

What did Christ say to the thief who prayed unto him?

He said unto him, "To-day shalt thou be with me in paradise." Luke 23 : 43.

 Stretched on the cross, the Saviour dies
 Hark! his expiring groans arise;
 See, from his hands, his feet, his side,
 Descends the sacred crimson tide.

 And didst thou bleed?—for sinners bleed
 And could the sun behold the deed?
 No; he withdrew his cheering ray,
 And darkness veiled the mourning day.

LESSON XXVIII.

Crucifixion and Resurrection of Christ.

Ques. What other remarkable things occurred at the crucifixion of Christ?

Ans. There was an earthquake, the vail of the temple was rent in twain from top to bottom, and the rocks were rent. Matt. 27: 51.

What is an earthquake?

It is great shaking of the earth.

What is meant by the vail of the temple being rent in twain?

A certain vail or large cloth in the temple which separated the priest from the people during certain religious services, was torn from top to bottom.

Of what does this fact seem to be a type?

Of the great fact that Christ as our great high Priest, having offered himself as a sacrifice unto God for our sins, every man may now approach God for himself through the sacrifice of Christ, without the mediation of any earthly priest.

When the centurion saw these things what did he say?

He said, "Truly this was the Son of God." Matt 27: 54.

Who was this centurion?

He was in all probability, the officer who had command of the Roman soldiers on the occasion.

What act of cruelty was performed upon the body of Christ after he was dead?

The soldier pierced his side with a spear, and there ran out blood and water. John 19 : 34.

Who buried Christ?

Joseph, of Arimathea, who was a disciple of Christ, and a rich man, and a counsellor. Matt. 27 : 57, Luke 23 : 50.

How did Joseph obtain the body of Christ?

He begged it of Pilot. Matt. 27 : 58.

How was the body of Christ buried?

Joseph wrapped it in a clean linen cloth, and laid it in his own new tomb, which he had hewn out of a rock, and rolled a great stone at the door. Matt. 27 : 59, 60.

Who assisted Joseph in the burial of Christ?

Nicodemus, who came to Jesus by night to converse with him. He brought myrrh and aloes, which were used in the burial. John 19 : 39, 40.

What request did the chief priests and Pharisees make of Pilot in regard to the tomb in which Christ was laid?

That it be made sure for three days, least the body of Christ should be taken away by his disciples, and they should then report that he had risen from the dead. Matt. 27 : 64,

What did Pilot do, in compliance with the request?

He directed them to have a watch, and

to make the sepulchre sure, which they did. v's 65, 66.

Who composed the watch which was set over the tomb of Jesus?

They were Roman soldiers.

How long did the body of Christ lay in the tomb?

From Friday afternoon until very early Sabbath morning, according to our days of the week; but according to the Jewish days, it was from Saturday till Monday.

What day do christians keep as Sabbath?

The day in which Christ arose from the dead, which is the first day of the week.

What is the meaning of Sabbath?

It means rest.

What is the proper name of the day which we call Sabbath, and how should it be observed?

The proper name is *Lord's Day*, and it should be observed by christians as a day in which to assemble for the public worship of God.

What was the Jewish Sabbath in memory of?

It was in memory of the completion of creation. God made all things in six days, and rested the seventh.

What is the Lord's Day, as kept by christians, in memory of?

It is in memory of the resurrection of Christ, which is the completion of redemption.

Unto whom did Christ first appear after he had risen from the dead?

Unto Mary Magdalene, out of whom he had cast seven devils. Luke 19: 9, ch. 8: 2.

Unto whom else did he appear?

Unto the eleven apostles, Luke 16: 14, and after that he was seen of above five hundred brethren at once. 1 Cor 15: 9.

What remarkable thing took place at the resurrection of Christ?

"The graves were opened, and many bodies of the saints which slept arose, and came out of the graves after his resurrection, and went into the holy city, and appeared unto many." Mat 27: 52, 53.

Why did Christ die and rise from the dead?

"Thus it behoved Christ to suffer, and to rise from the dead the third day; and that repentance and remission of sins should be preached in his name among all nations, beginning at Jerusalem." Luke 24: 46, 47.

He dies! the friend of sinners dies!
Lo! Salem's daughters weep around;
A solemn darkness veils the skies,
A sudden trembling shakes the ground.

Come, saints, and drop a tear or two
For him who groaned beneath your load;
He shed a thousand drops for you,
A thousand drops of richer blood.

Here's love and grief beyond degree,
The Lord of Glory dies for men!

But lo! what sudden jows we see,
  Jesus the dead revives again!

The rising God forsakes the tomb!
  Up to his Father's court he flies;
Cherubic legions guard him home,
  And shout him welcome to the skies.

Break off your tears, ye saints, and tell
  How high our great Deliverer reigns;
Sing how he spoiled the hosts of hell,
  And led the monster Death in chains.

Say, "Live forever, wondrous King!
  Born to redeem, and strong to save!"
Then ask, "O death, where is thy sting?"
And, "Where's thy victory, boasting grave?"

LESSON XXIX.

Christ after his Resurrection.

Ques. Where did Christ promise to meet his disciples after his resurrection?

Ans. In Galilee, his native country. Matt. 26: 32, and 28: 6.

What remarkable circumstance occurred on the day of Christ's resurrection, between Jerusalem and Emmaus?

Christ joined himself in company with two of his disciples who were sad, and were talking over the things which had happened to him. Luke 24: 13—29.

Did these disciples know Christ?

They did not, but supposed that he was a stranger in Jerusalem. v. 18.

What did Christ do while in company with these two disciples?

He expounded the Scriptures unto them, showing the necessity of his sufferings and death. verses 25—27.

When did Christ make himself known unto these disciples?

When he sat down with them to meat, and took bread, and blessed it, and brake, and gave unto them, according to his usual custom. verses 30, 31.

What may we learn from this narrative?

That Christ is often nearer to his people while they are talking or meditating of him, than they think he is.

What may we farther learn from this narrative?

That it is good for those who love Christ to talk and to meditate of him.

What did these disciples say one to another after Christ made himself known unto them?

They said, "Did not our heart burn within us while he talked with us by the way, and while he opened to us the Scriptures?" v. 32.

What is meant here by "the Scriptures?"

The writings of the Old Testament.

What did these two disciples do after this?

They hastened back to Jerusalem to tell the eleven apostles that Christ had risen from the dead. verses 33—35.

While these disciples were telling the others what things they had seen and heard, what happened?

"Jesus himself stood in the midst of them, and said unto them, Peace unto you." v. 36.

How were the disciples affected at this sudden manifestation of Christ?

They were terrified and affrightened, and supposed that they had seen a spirit." v. 37.

Which of the disciples was absent on this occasion?

Thomas, who is called Didymus. John 20: 24.

How was Thomas affected when the disciples told him that the Lord had risen from the dead and that they had seen him?

He did not believe them; and said he would not believe unless he saw and put his fingers in the prints of the nails, and his hand into the side of Christ. John 20: 25.

When did Christ next appear unto his disciples?

After eight days. v. 29.

Was Thomas present on this occasion?

He was.

What did Christ say unto him?

He said unto him, "Reach hither thy finger, and behold my hands; and reach hither thy hand, and thrust into my side; and be not faithless, but believing." v. 27.

What did Thomas then say?

He said, "My Lord and my God." v. 28.

What did Christ then say ?

He said, "Blessed are they that have not seen, and yet have believed." v. 29.

Have you seen Christ? and do you believe in him?

What do we receive in consequence of faith in Christ?

We have life through his name. v. 31.

At what place did Christ next meet with his disciples?

At the sea of Tiberias. John 21 : 1.

What remarkable thing took place there?

He caused Peter to confess him three times, who had denied him three times. John, chap. 21, Matt. 26 : 34.

How long did Christ remain on earth after his resurrection?

Forty days. Acts 1 : 3.

What was Christ's last command to his disciples?

"Go ye into all the world, and preach the gospel to every creature. He that believeth and is baptized shall be saved; but he that believeth not shall be damned."

Do you believe in Christ? and if so, have you been baptized since you believed?

> Go preach my gospel," saith the Lord;
> "Bid the whole earth my grace receive;
> He shall be saved that trusts my word,
> And he condemned who'll not believe.
>
> I'll make your great commission known;
> And ye shall prove my gospel true,
> By all the works that I have done,
> By all the wonders ye shall do.
>
> "Teach all the nations my commands:

I'm with you till the world shall end;
All power is trusted in my hands;
I can destroy, and I defend."

He spake, and light shone round his head;
On a bright cloud to heaven he rode:
They to the farthest nations spread
The grace of their ascended God.

LESSON XXX.

Ascension and intercession of Christ.

Ques. From what place did Christ ascend to heaven?

Ans. Luke says he ascended from Bethany, Luke 24: 50, and also from mount Olivet. Acts 1: 12.

How can these two statements be reconciled?

Bethany was situated on mount Olivet, so that when he was in Bethany he was also on the mountain.

What was Christ's last act before he ascended to heaven?

Blessing his disciples. "And it came to pass, while he blessed them, he was parted from them, and carried up into heaven. Luke 24: 51.

How did Christ ascend to heaven?

It seems that he arose from the earth some distance, and was then received into a cloud and so passed out of sight. Acts 1: 9.

What was this cloud into which Christ was received!

It was, in all probability, a multitude of angels, who had descended from heaven, and were poised in the air, waiting to receive Christ and conduct him up into heaven with great honor.

What are the conducting angels represented by David to have said on this occasion?

"Lift up your heads, O ye gates; and be ye lifted up ye everlasting doors; and the King of glory shall come in." Psalm 24.

What was the response to this?

"Who is this King of glory?"

What reply was made to this?

"The Lord strong and mighty, the Lord mighty in battle; the Lord of hosts, he is the king of glory."

Who appeared unto the disciples as they stood gazing up into heaven at the ascension of Christ?

"Two men stood by them in white apparel." Acts 1: 10.

What were these two men?

They were angels.

What promise did these two angels make to the disciples?

That this same Jesus whom they had seen ascend into heaven should return again in like manner as they had seen him ascend. Acts 1: 11.

Where is Christ now?

He is exalted at the right hand of God

the Father, to be a Prince and a Saviour. Acts 5: 31, Heb. 12: 2.

What is his peculiar work there?

To give repentance and remission of sins. Acts 5: 31, Col. 1: 14.

How do we receive remission of sins by Christ?

By his intercessions. He is continually making intercessions for his people. Heb. 7: 25.

What are we to understand by the intercession of Christ?

Having made full atonement for the sins of his people, by enduring in his own person that penalty which was due to their sins, his presence at the right hand of the Father, continually shows the reason why those should be forgiven who come to God in his name.

By what other name is Christ called as our intercessor?

He is called our Advocate. "If any man sin, we have an advocate with the Father, Jesus Christ the rightous." 1 John 2: 1.

What is the business of an Advocate?

To show cause why those should be aquitted for whom he pleads.

For whom does Christ plead?

For his people.

Of what are his people to be aquitted?

Of the guilt of sin.

Are his people sinners?
They are, but sinners saved by grace.
What is the ground of his pleadings?
That he died for their sins, and arose for their justification.

He lives! the great Redeemer lives!
What joy the blest assurance gives!
And now before his Father God,
He pleads the merits of his blood.

Repeated crimes awake our fears,
And justice armed with frowns appears;
But in the Saviour's lovely face
Sweet mercy smiles, and all is peace.

Hence, then ye dark, despairing thoughts;
Above our fears, above our faults,
His powerful intercessions rise;
And guilt recedes, and terror dies.

Great Advocate, almighty Friend.
On thee our humble hopes depend;
Our cause can never, never fail,
For thou dost plead, and must prevail.

www.ingramcontent.com/pod-product-compliance
Lightning Source LLC
Chambersburg PA
CBHW031406160426
43196CB00007B/921